THE COMPLETELY DIFFERENT WORLD OF PROTISTS

Biology Book for Kids
Children's Biology Books

BABY PROFESSOR

EDUCATION KIDS

In this book, we're going to cover the interesting and different world of protists. So, let's get right to it.

Euglena

There are millions upon millions of animal and plant species on Earth. Scientists use a complex system to categorize them. The top level of this system is called the **kingdoms** and there are six kingdoms. Protists is one of those kingdoms.

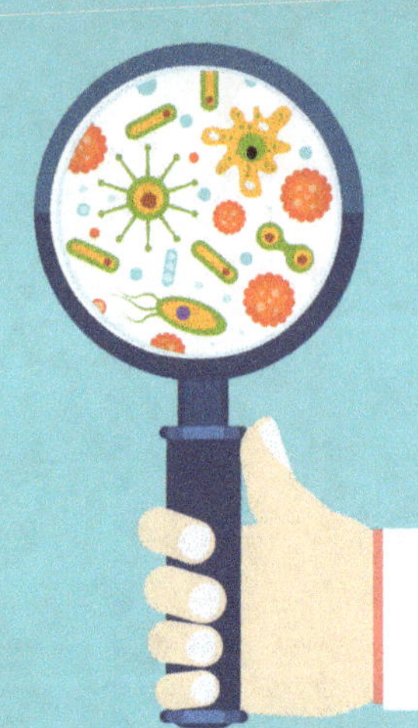

Unlike bacteria, which have very simple cells, protists have eukaryotic cells. This simply means that their cells have a "command center" called the nucleus and other organelles in their cells. Most protists are unicellular, but not all of them are. Protists are not animals. They're not plants or fungi either. They fall into a category all their own. In fact, you can think of them as all the eukaryotic organisms that do NOT fall into the category of animals, plants, or fungi. Protozoa, algae, and slime molds fall into the category of protists.

Stentor

Ernst Haeckel

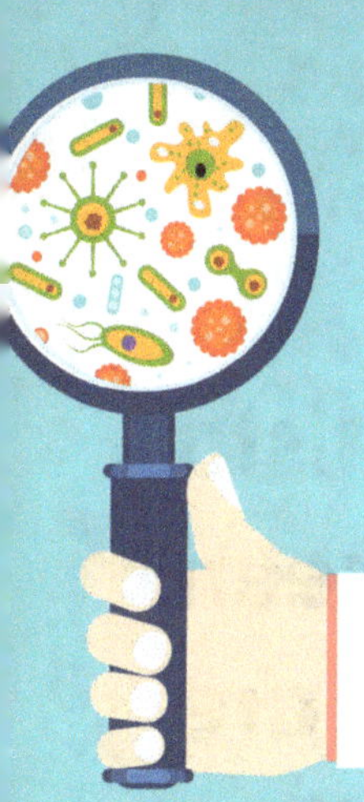

THE KINGDOM PROTISTA

In 1866, when the German biologist Ernst Haeckel first proposed the Kingdom Protista, it wasn't accepted. In fact, it wasn't accepted as a classification until the 1960s. The reason is that the organisms in this kingdom are so diverse from each other. In some cases, all they have in common is that they are NOT plants, animals, or fungi. It's been nicknamed the "junk drawer" kingdom for that reason.

Most organisms in the Kingdom Protista are so tiny that they can only be seen using a microscope. There are a few that are multicellular, which simply means that they have many cells. The multicellular protists can get rather large. **Kelp** is a good example of a multicellular protist. If you've ever seen a big piece or pieces of kelp that have washed up on the beach you know how big it can get. Some of them grow to over 100 meters in length. The cells in kelp all look the same. They are eukaryotic cells but they don't differ in function from each other like the cells in your body do.

Giant kelp

Desmids

If you were drawing a diagram and you had bacteria on one side because it has simple cells, and animals and plants on the other because their cells are complex and specialized, protists would fall right in the middle. They have cells that each contain a nucleus, but most of them don't have cells that have specialized tasks.

CHARACTERISTICS OF PROTISTS

There are a few common characteristics of protists.

They have **eukaryotic cells**, which means that each of their cells has a nucleus.

Most of them have mitochondria. These organelles absorb nutrients and transform them into energy for the cell.

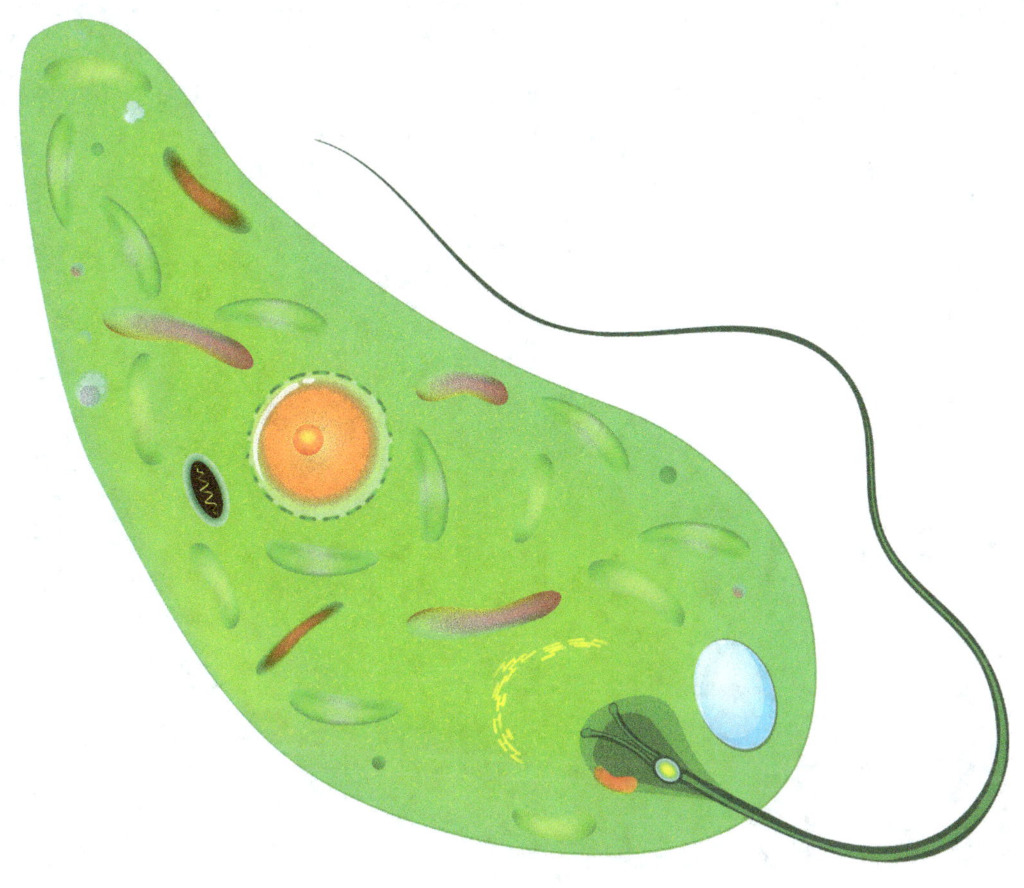

Euglena is a single-celled flagellate Eukaryotes.

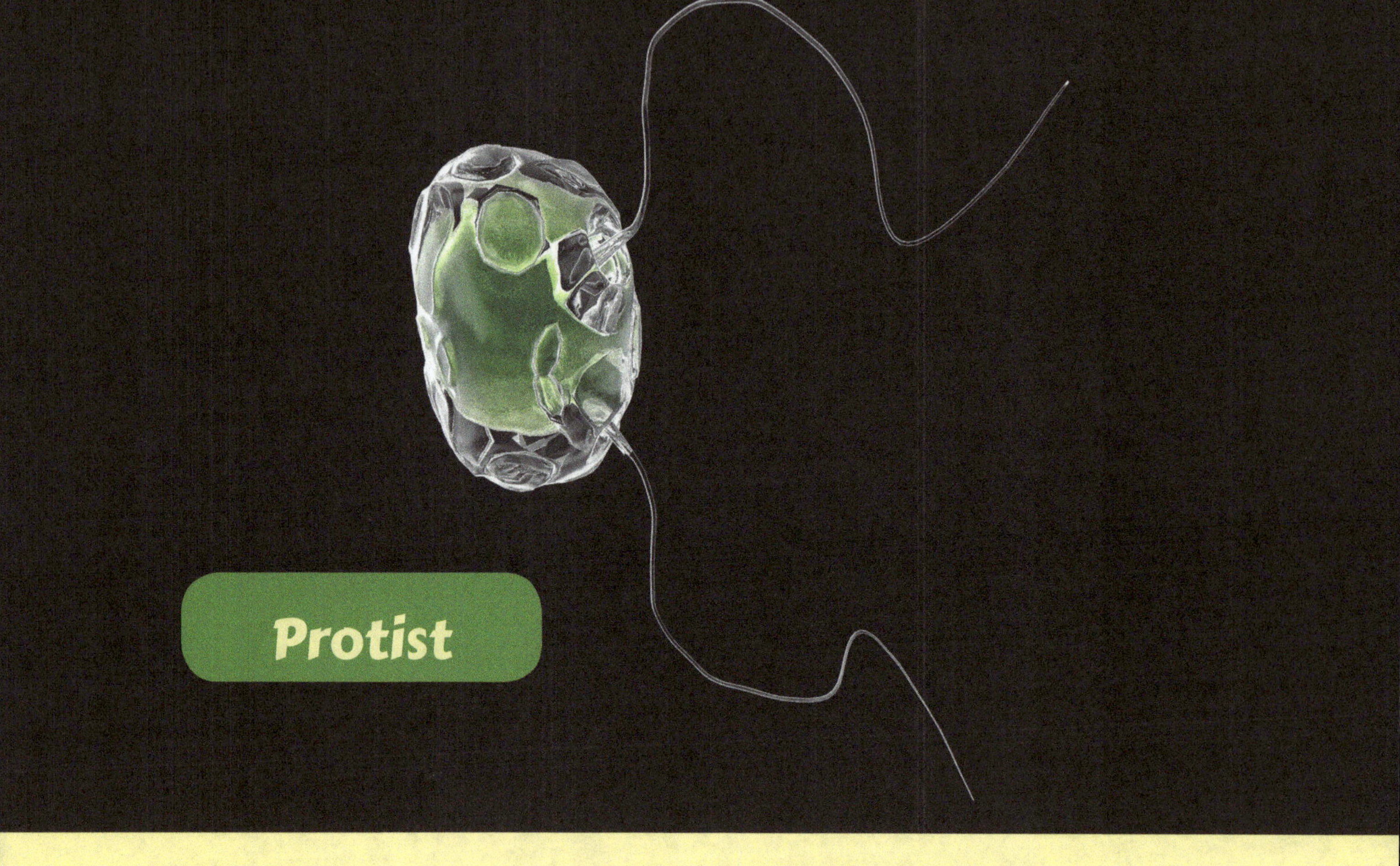

Protists are sometimes parasites. The organism that causes malaria is a protist.

They prefer aquatic environments, but many species can be found in moist soil.

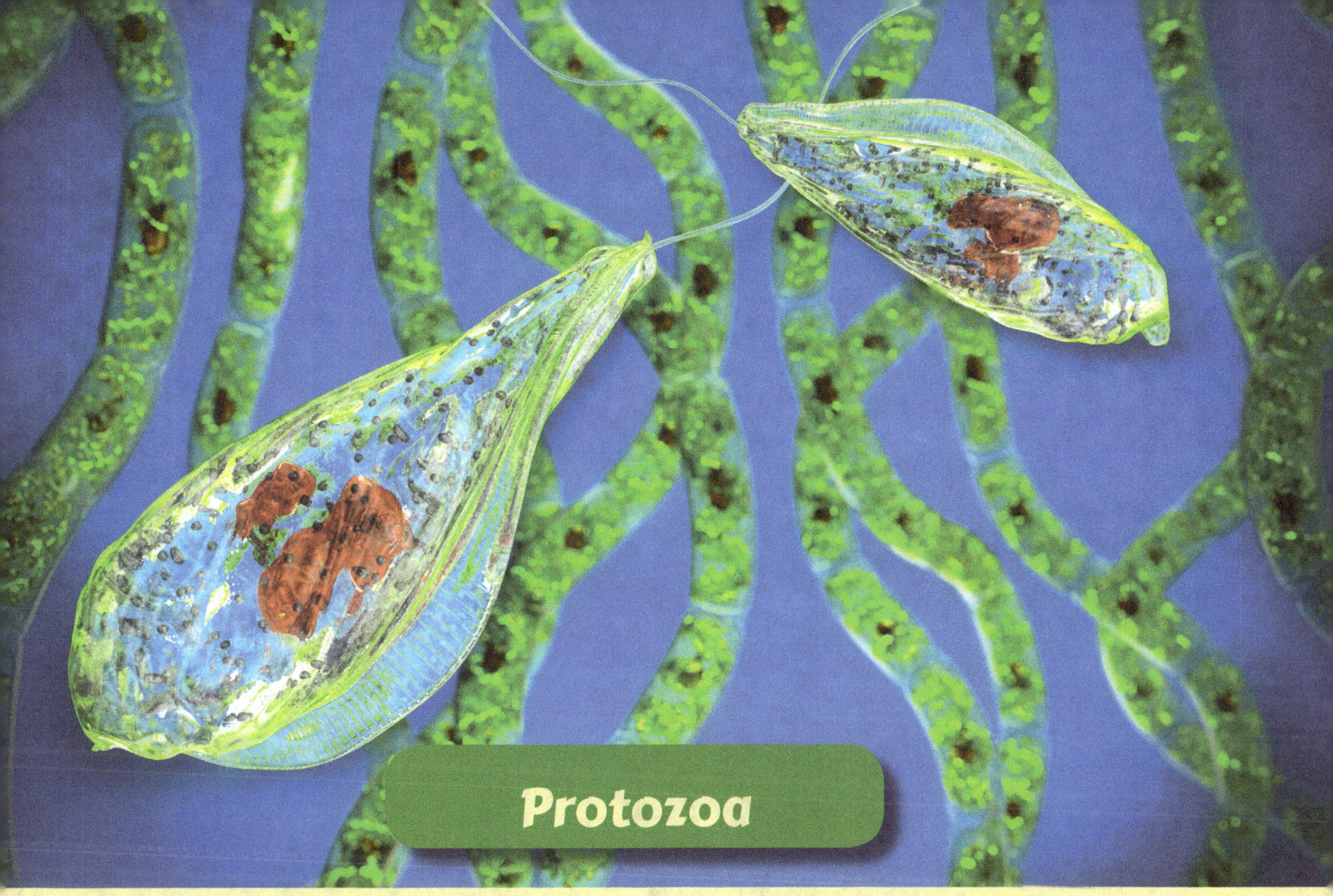

The protists are a huge category of organisms and scientists are still actively organizing them. They are divided into three main groups based on how similar they are to the animal, plant and fungi kingdoms.

Slime mold, a fungi-like protist

CLASSIFICATION OF PROTISTS

One way that protists can be categorized is by how similar they are to animals, plants, or fungi.

Animal-like protists, which have the ability to move and must eat other organisms for food

Plant-like protists, which can create their own food through photosynthesis

Fungi-like protists, which reproduce by using spores and can't create their own food

There are thousands of species that fall into the Kingdom Protista. These are major categories of the organisms that are generally classified there.

PROTISTA

Algae

THREE OF THE LARGE CATEGORIES OF PROTISTS

Protozoa, which are animal-like protists
Algae, which are plant-like protists
Slime Molds, which are fungi-like protists

HOW PROTISTS MOVE

Another way that biologists categorize protists is by the way they move. Different types of protozoa use these three different methods of moving.

Flagella: These are long, whip-like appendages. Some protozoa have several and some only have one. These flagella help the organism move back and forth.

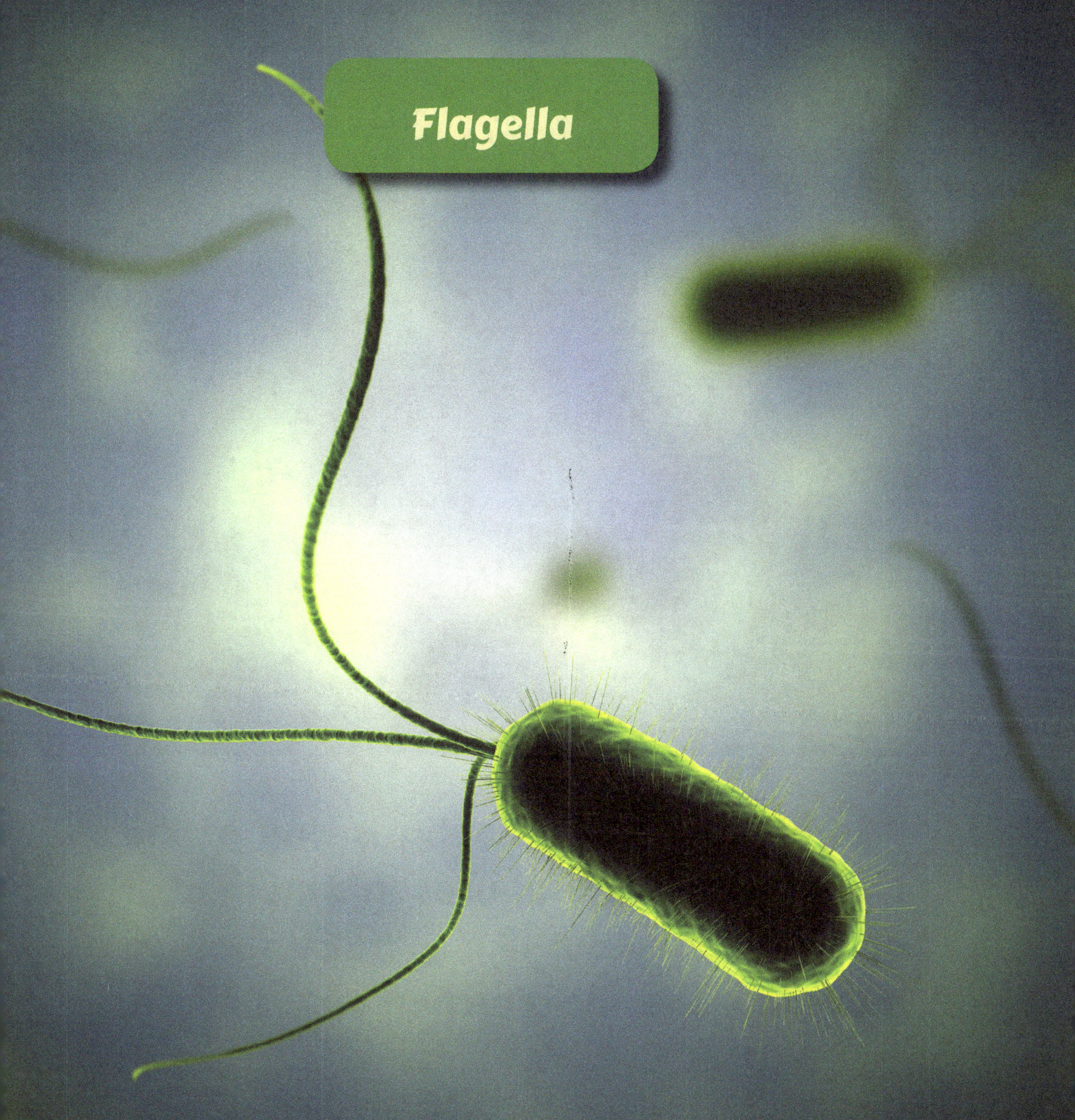

Flagella

Pseudopodia: An amoeba is one of the types of protists that uses this method. It oozes its body out like a "false foot" to move in a specific direction on a surface.

Cilia: Some protozoa use tiny hair-like structures called cilia to move. The cilia move in a wave-like pattern to help the organism move backward and forward.

PROTOZOA

Protozoa can be single-celled or multi-celled. Like animals, they track down their food in the environment they are swimming in or moving in. They can be found in freshwater, such as ponds and rivers, marine habitats, and in the soil. They are microscopic.

Paramecium and amoeba protozoa

Paramecium

There are so many different species of protozoa. They are very diverse, which means that they differ in how they move, what they eat, their shape, and their size.

Biologists classify them into four different groups: the amoebas, the sporozoans, the ciliates, and the flagellates.

Amoebas produce long extensions of their bodies called **pseudopods**. When they find a particle of food they want they surround the food with their pseudopod and then they absorb it. Next, they digest it by using special enzymes that break down the food. Another interesting fact about amoebas is that if you divide one in half, the half with the nucleus lives but the other half dies.

Pseudopods

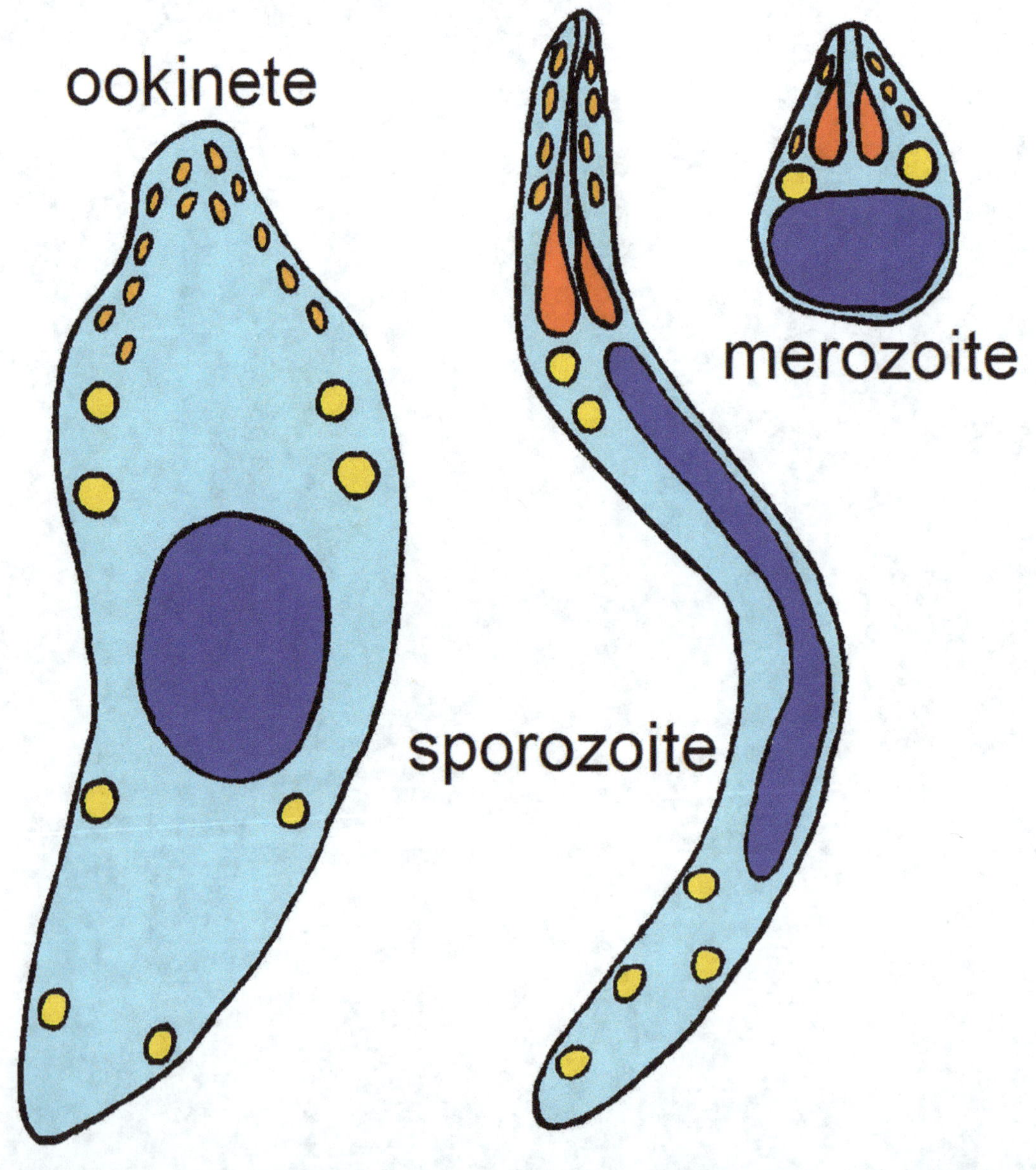

Sporozoans

Sporozoans don't have a way to move by themselves since they don't have flagella, cilia, or pseudopodia. They must live inside a human or animal host as a parasite. These organisms cause disease.

A paramecium is an example of a ciliate. As its cilia move back and forth, they cause the paramecium to move forward while it is spinning.

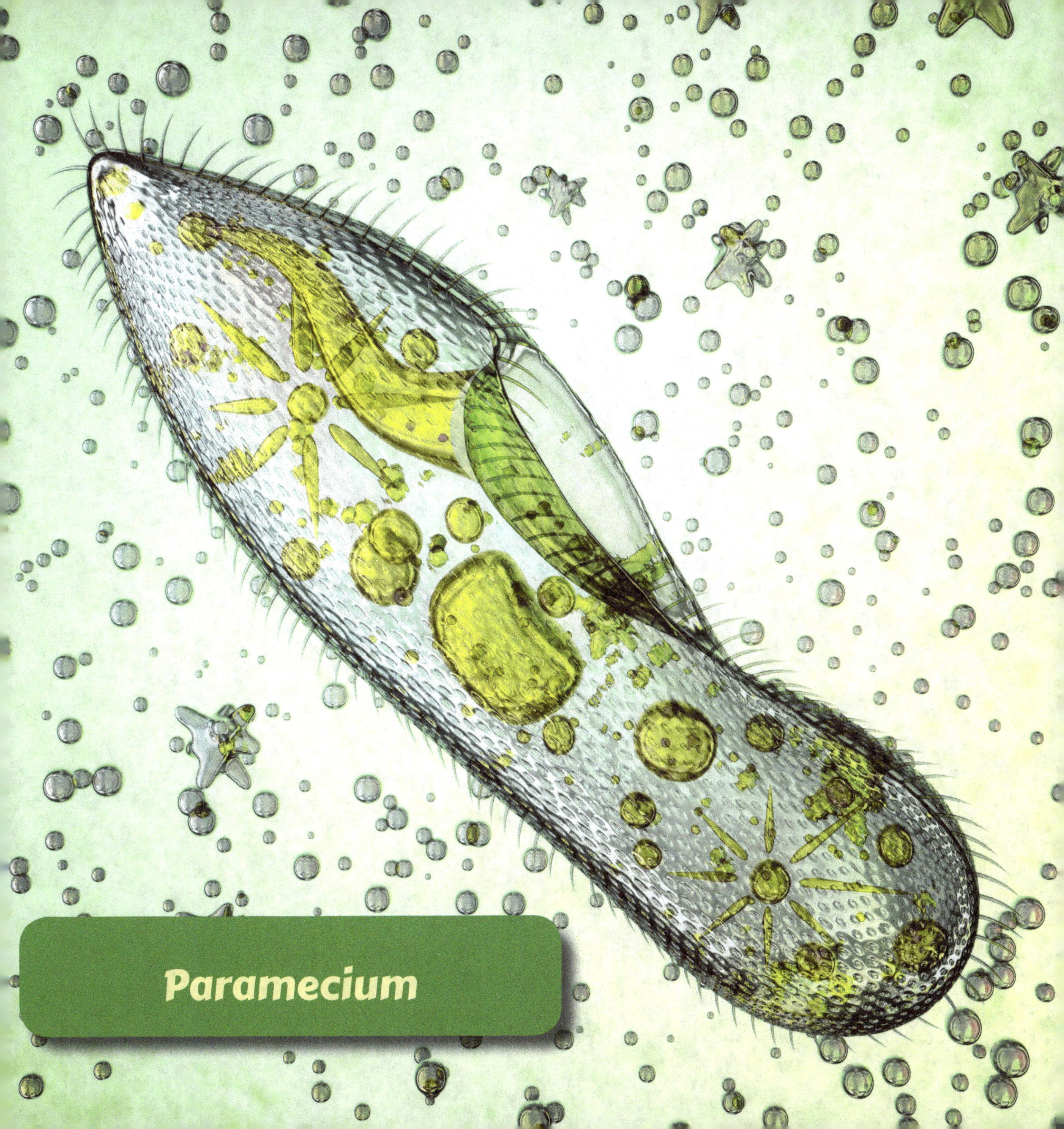
Paramecium

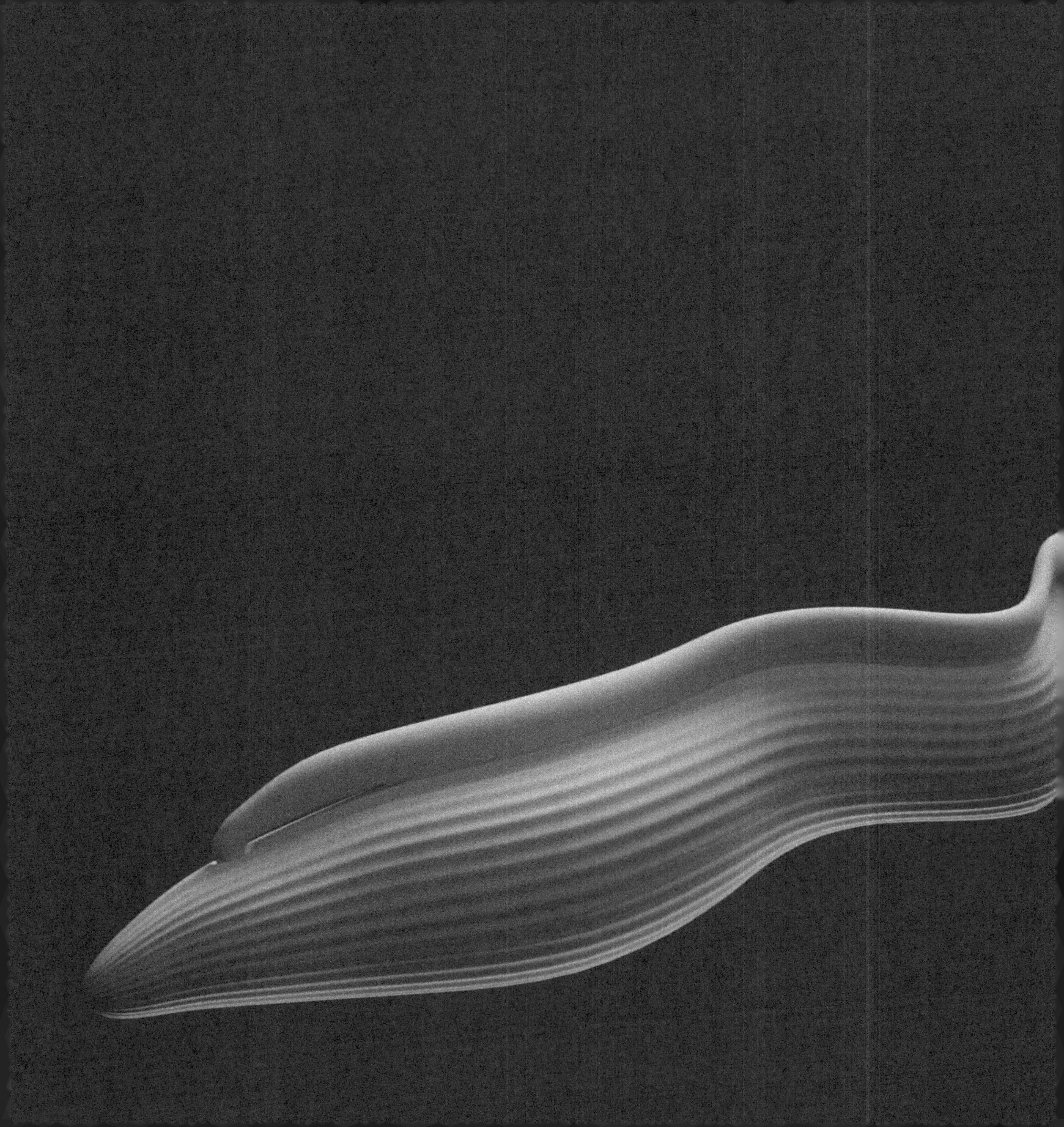

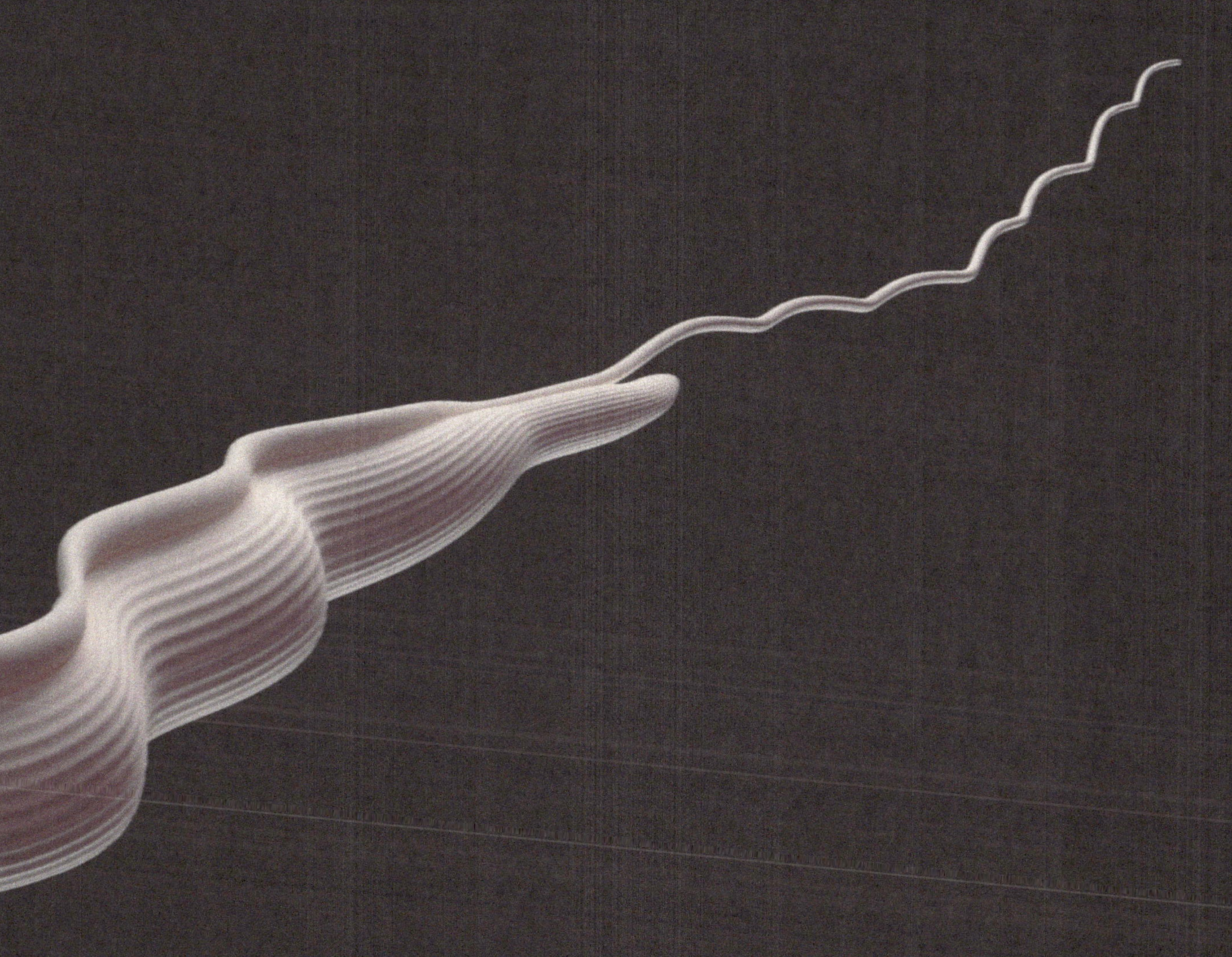

A **Trypanosoma brucei** is an example of a protozoan flagellate. It uses its whip-like flagella to move.

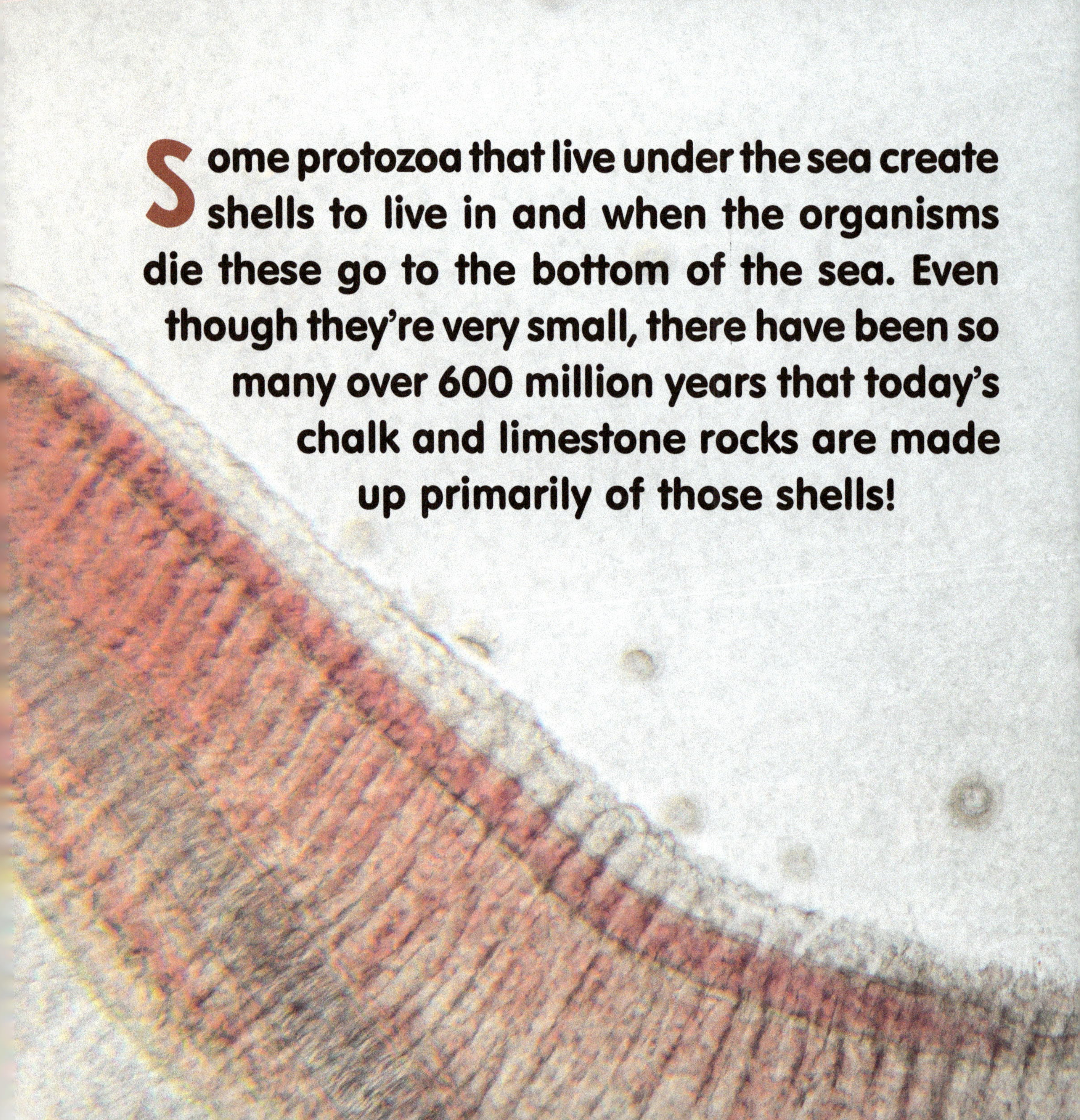
Some protozoa that live under the sea create shells to live in and when the organisms die these go to the bottom of the sea. Even though they're very small, there have been so many over 600 million years that today's chalk and limestone rocks are made up primarily of those shells!

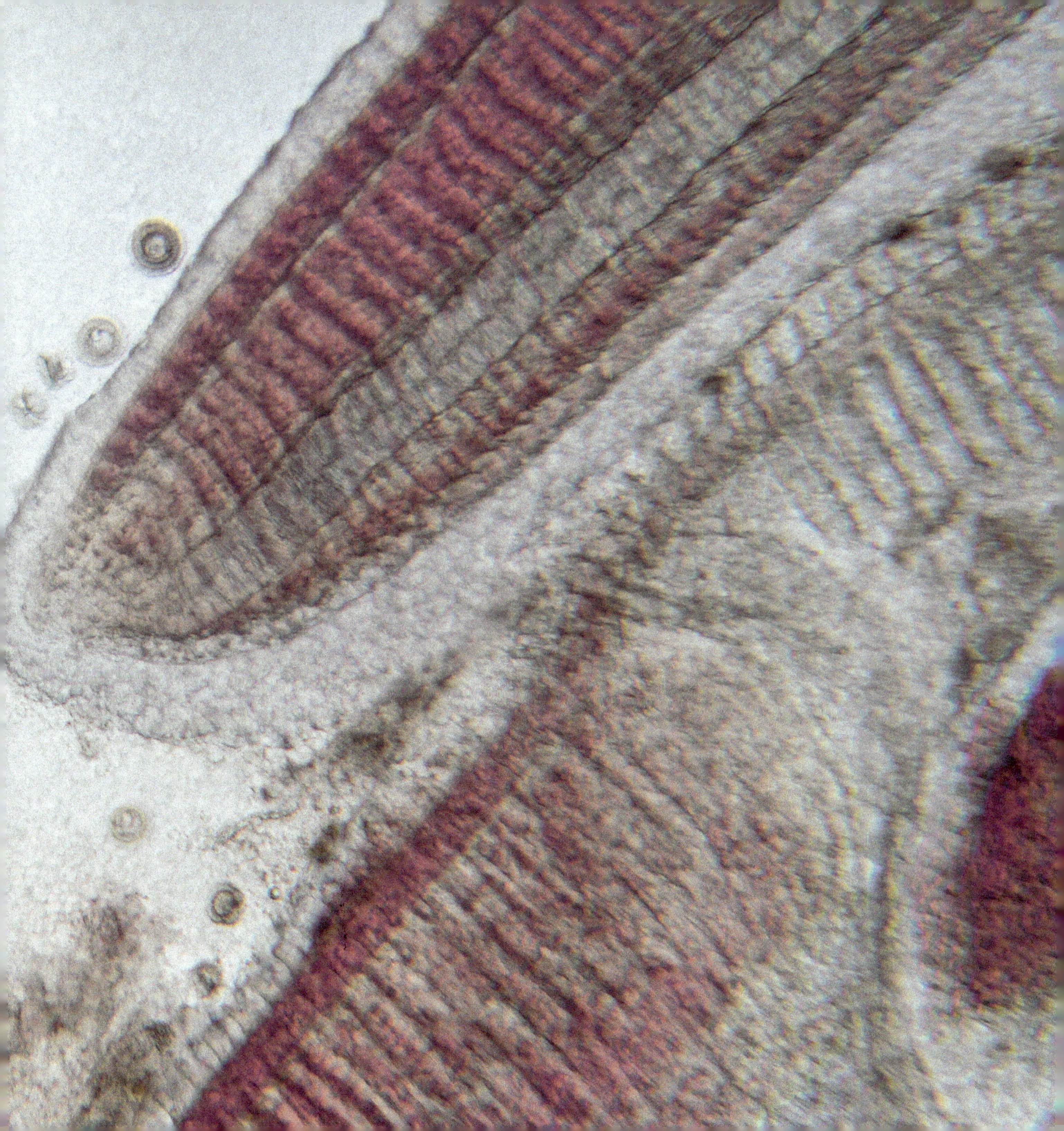

Algae

ALGAE, IS IT A PLANT OR A PROTIST?

Algae are sometimes categorized to be part of the plant kingdom and sometimes they are considered to be protists. According to some recent studies of evolutionary relationships, red algae and also green algae are most closely connected to plants. However, there are other types of algae that seem to be more closely related to certain groups within the protists.

New algae are discovered all the time, and as scientists learn more about them classifications may change. The scientists who feel that algae aren't plants argue that plants have specialized tissues, such as stems, roots, and leaves, so they feel that algae belong in the "junk drawer" of protists.

Algae

Green algae in microscope

One thing is certain. If you classify algae as a protist, then it is definitely a plant-like protist since it makes its own food through photosynthesis. Algae contain chlorophyll, which is a green pigment that absorbs light to give the energy for photosynthesis. In other words, it's solar power in its most natural form. The many different types of algae are sometimes organized by their colors of green, brown, yellow, and red.

Nearly 50 percent of the photosynthesis on Earth is done by algae, so whether you consider them a plant or a protist, algae are critical to the environment.

Slime molds

SLIME MOLDS

Slime molds are not the same types of molds that fall into the fungi category. The slime molds that are protists fall into two categories: cellular slime molds and plasmodial slime molds.

Cellular slime molds are small and uni-cellular, which means they have one cell. However, to make the mold they work together as if they were a single organism.

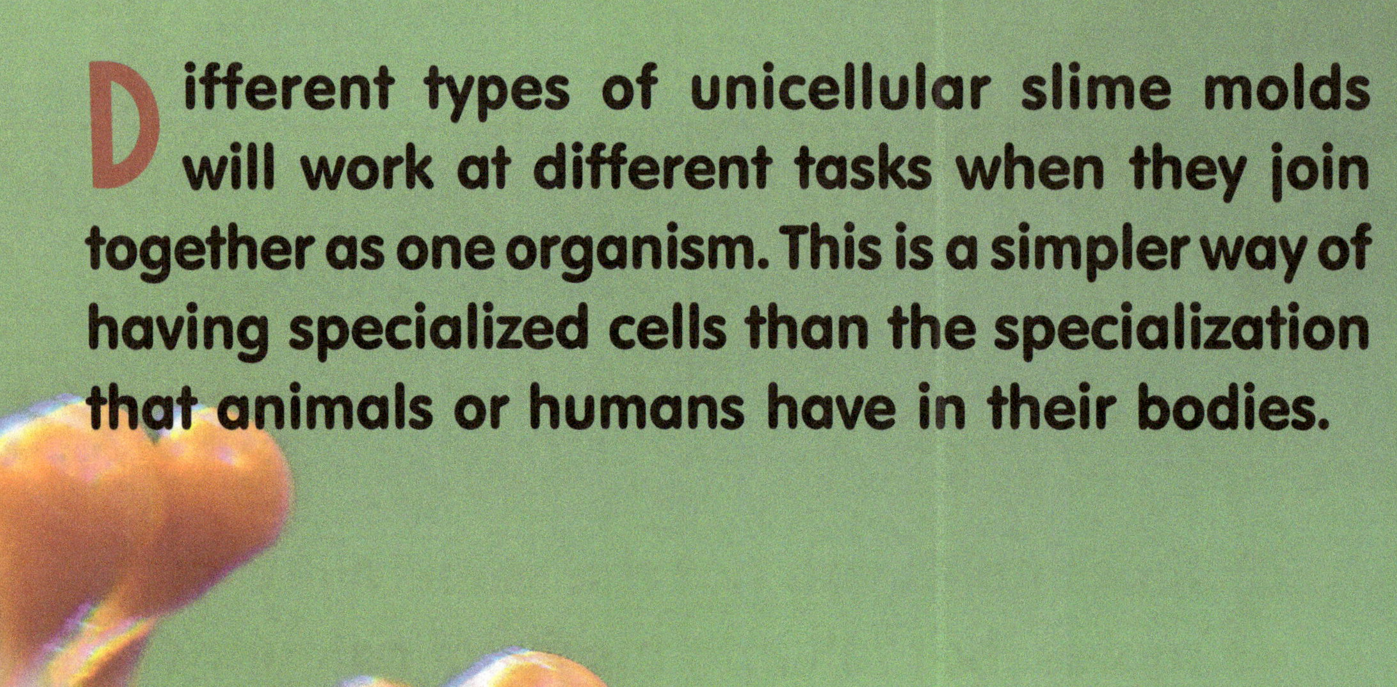

Different types of unicellular slime molds will work at different tasks when they join together as one organism. This is a simpler way of having specialized cells than the specialization that animals or humans have in their bodies.

Plasmodial slime molds are the opposite of cellular slime molds. They are just made from one cell. Even though they're only one cell they can get several feet in width. They can have more than one nucleus as a "command center" in their one cell as well.

PROTISTS AND DISEASES

Unfortunately, protists are responsible for some serious human diseases.

In East Africa, a person who is bitten by the Tsetse Fly may get the dreaded Sleeping Sickness. The Tsetse Fly carries the Trypanosoma brucei protozoa and when it bites the person it transfers this deadly parasite.

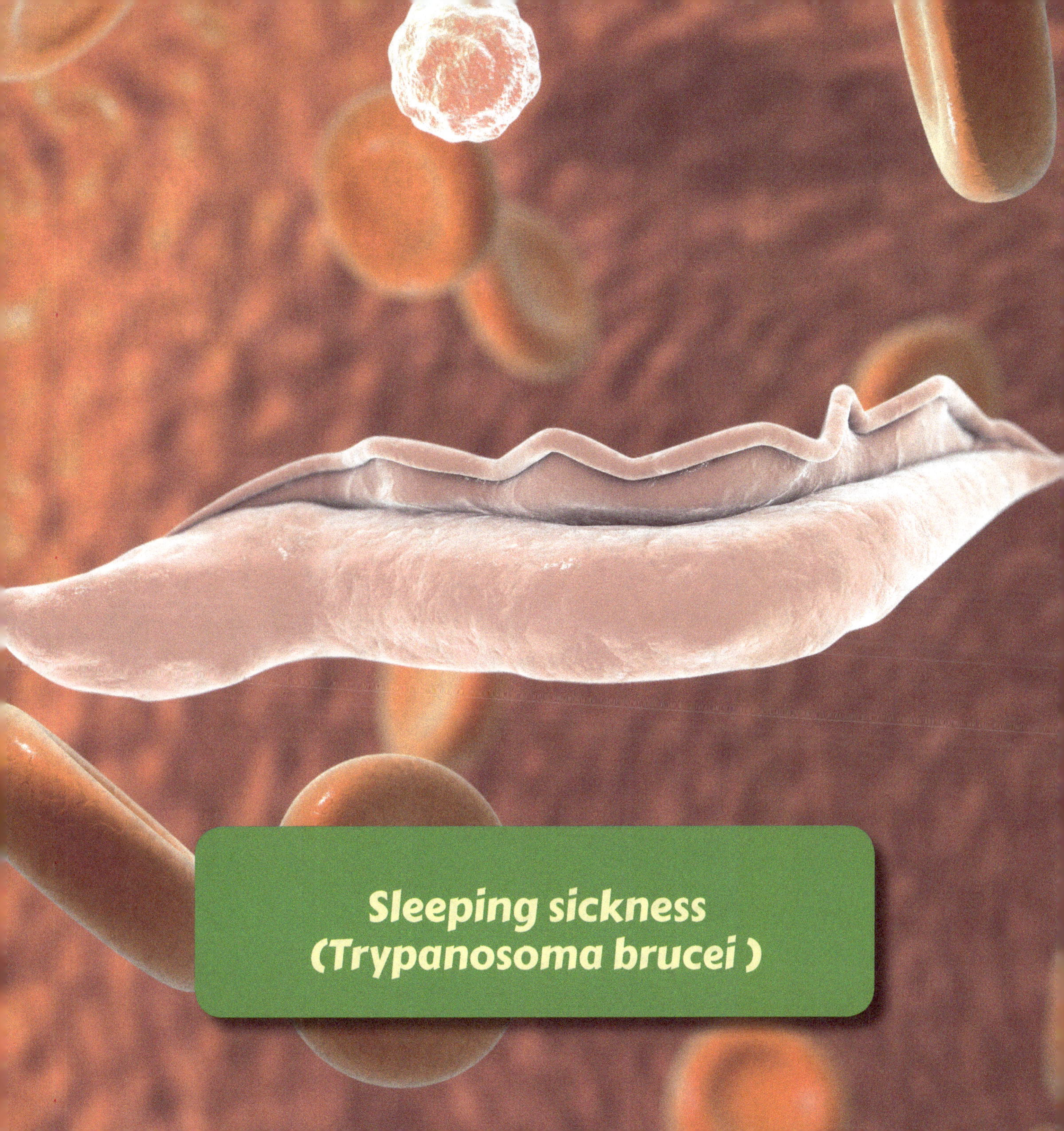

Sleeping sickness
(Trypanosoma brucei)

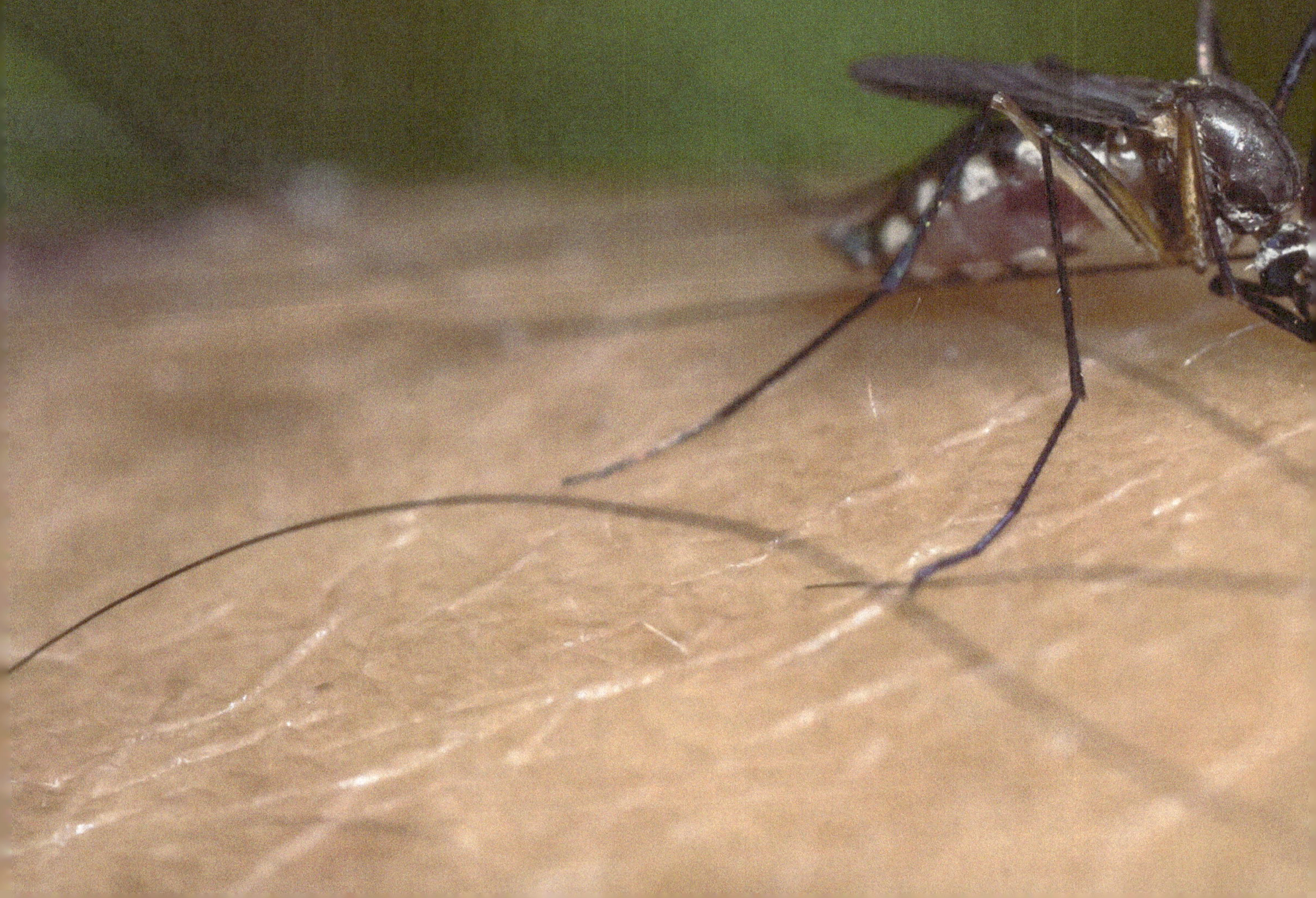
The most serious disease caused by protozoa is malaria. It's caused by Plasmodium. They are parasites of humans as well as mosquitoes. Malaria kills over one million people annually, many of them are children in Africa.

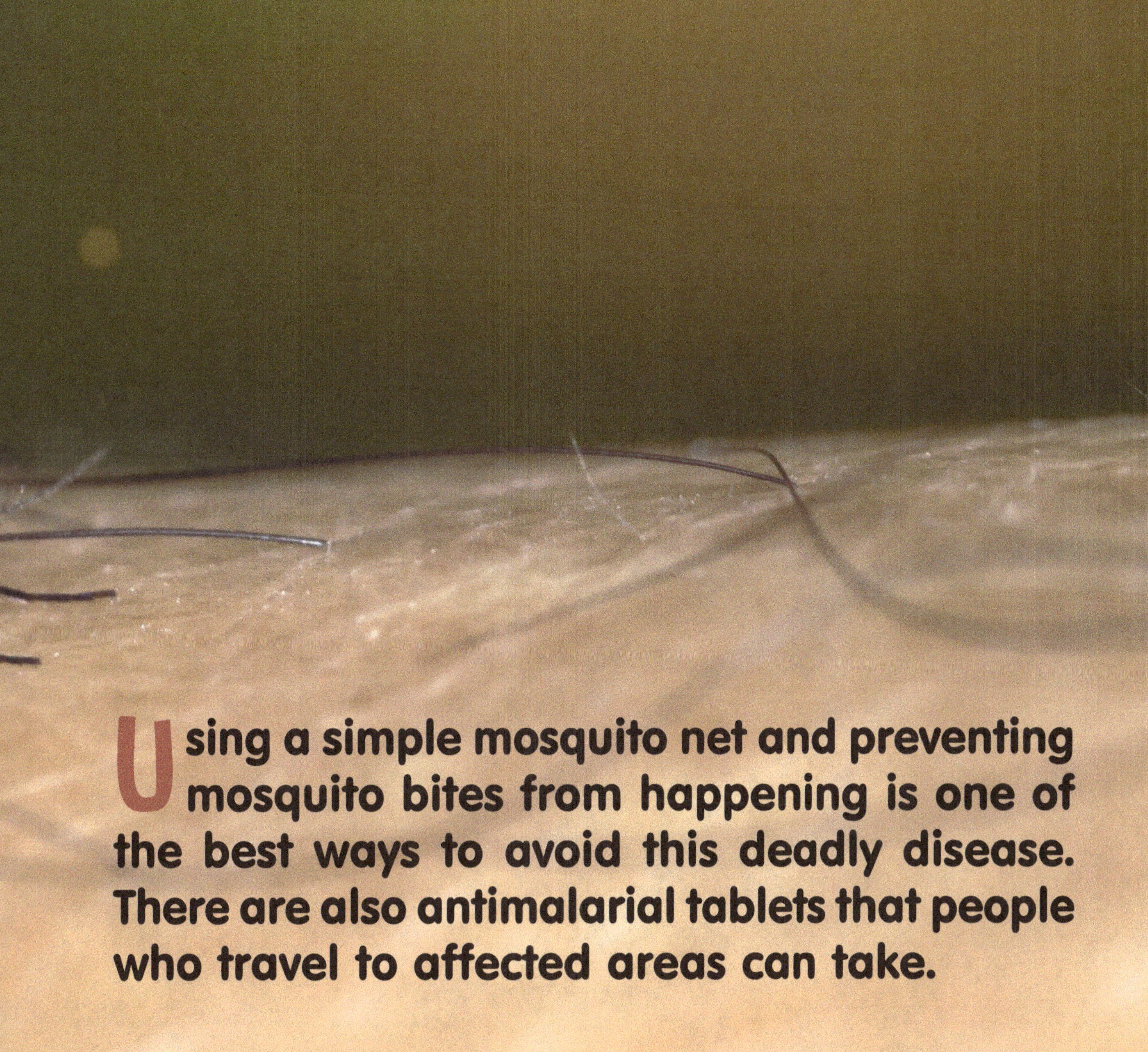

Using a simple mosquito net and preventing mosquito bites from happening is one of the best ways to avoid this deadly disease. There are also antimalarial tablets that people who travel to affected areas can take.

Now you know more about the diverse collection of organisms called the protists. You can find more Biology Books from Baby Professor by searching the website of your favorite book retailer.

Visit
BABY PROFESSOR
EDUCATION KIDS
www.BabyProfessorBooks.com
to download Free Baby Professor eBooks
and view our catalog of new and exciting
Children's Books

www.ingramcontent.com/pod-product-compliance
Lightning Source LLC
Chambersburg PA
CBHW080745180726
48003CB00021B/2888

* 9 7 9 8 8 6 9 4 3 0 3 3 5 *